A Study of Hands

by

Kelly Sadler

Kelly Sadler is a Minnesota based artist, illustrator, and aspiring philanthropist. She has a BFA in illustration from the College of Visual Arts, St. Paul, MN, and a BS in Marketing from Metropolitan State University, St. Paul, MN. All drawings were produced by her, and reflect the uniqueness that we all present.

Copyright © 2018 by Kelly Sadler. All rights reserved. This book or any portion thereof shall not be reproduced or used in any manner whatsoever without the express written permission of the author and publisher except for the use of brief quotations for the purposes of book review.

First published, 2018.

ISBN-13: 978-1719505574

ISBN-10: 1719505578

Kelly Sadler
3817 Scott Ave. N
Robbinsdale, Mn 55422

To Mom:
Thank you for your artistic inspirations, encouragement, and love of the arts.

To Dad:
Thank you for your love of medicine, for not making me go into the medical field, and for leaving your medical journals out for me to dig through and find inspiration.

To Hubby:
Thank you for challenging me, pushing me, and never letting me walk away from things that feel too burdonsome at times.

To Kiddo:
Dreams can come true. You just have to be willing to work for it and make your success your own.

To my Grandmothers:
Thank you for your work, your grit, and your grace. Hopefully I can live up to all that you worked for.

The Story of Hands

I have always been fascinated by hands. They are the doers of our physical existence. Minds think and analyze, feet set our direction, but our hands carry out the work that needs to be done.

Simple, expressive, uncomplicated, clear. A tool to help us animate and express our ideas, bring life to our visions, sooth the aching heart, and heal that which is injured. So simple, but often times speak louder than mere words.

As you flip through the pages of this book, I sincerely hope that you glean as much enjoyment out of deciphering the stories as I had making them.

- Kelly

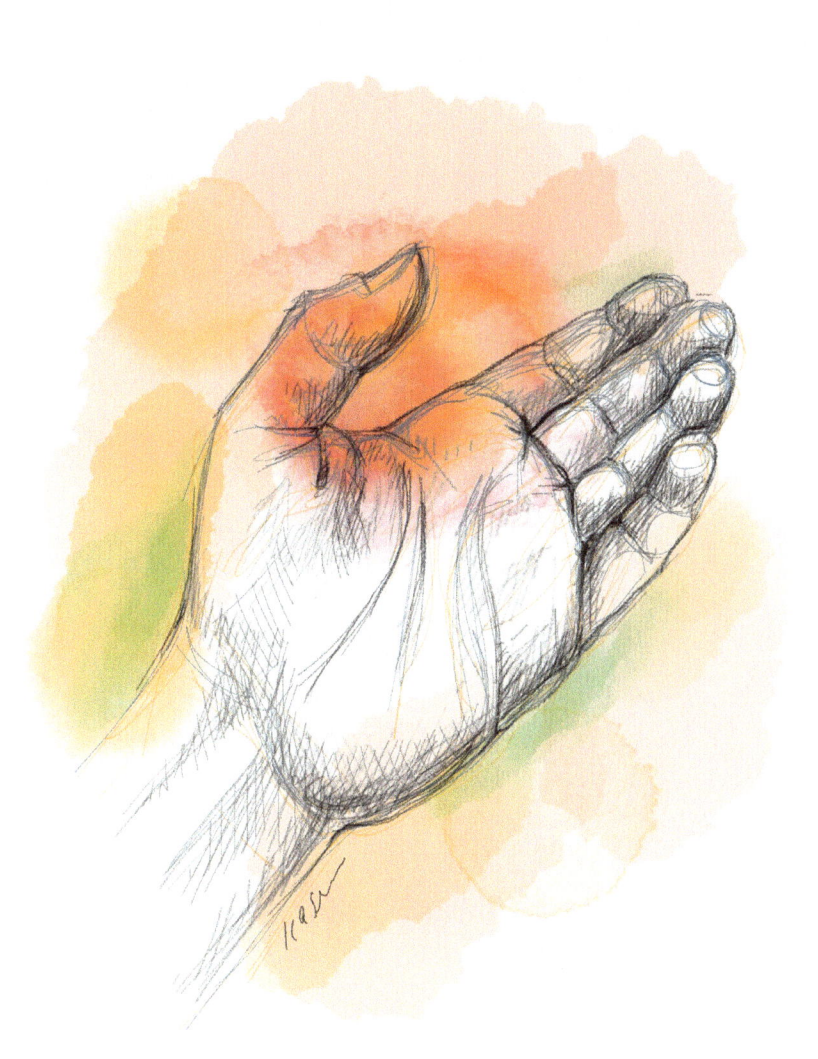

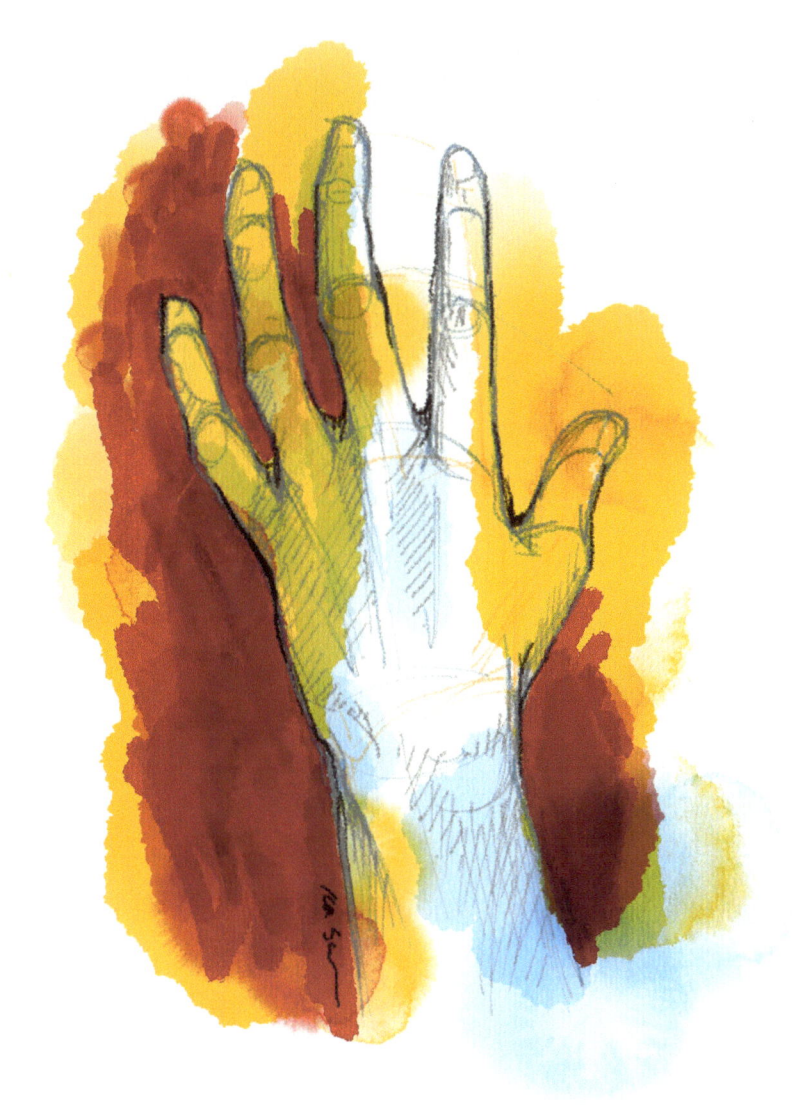

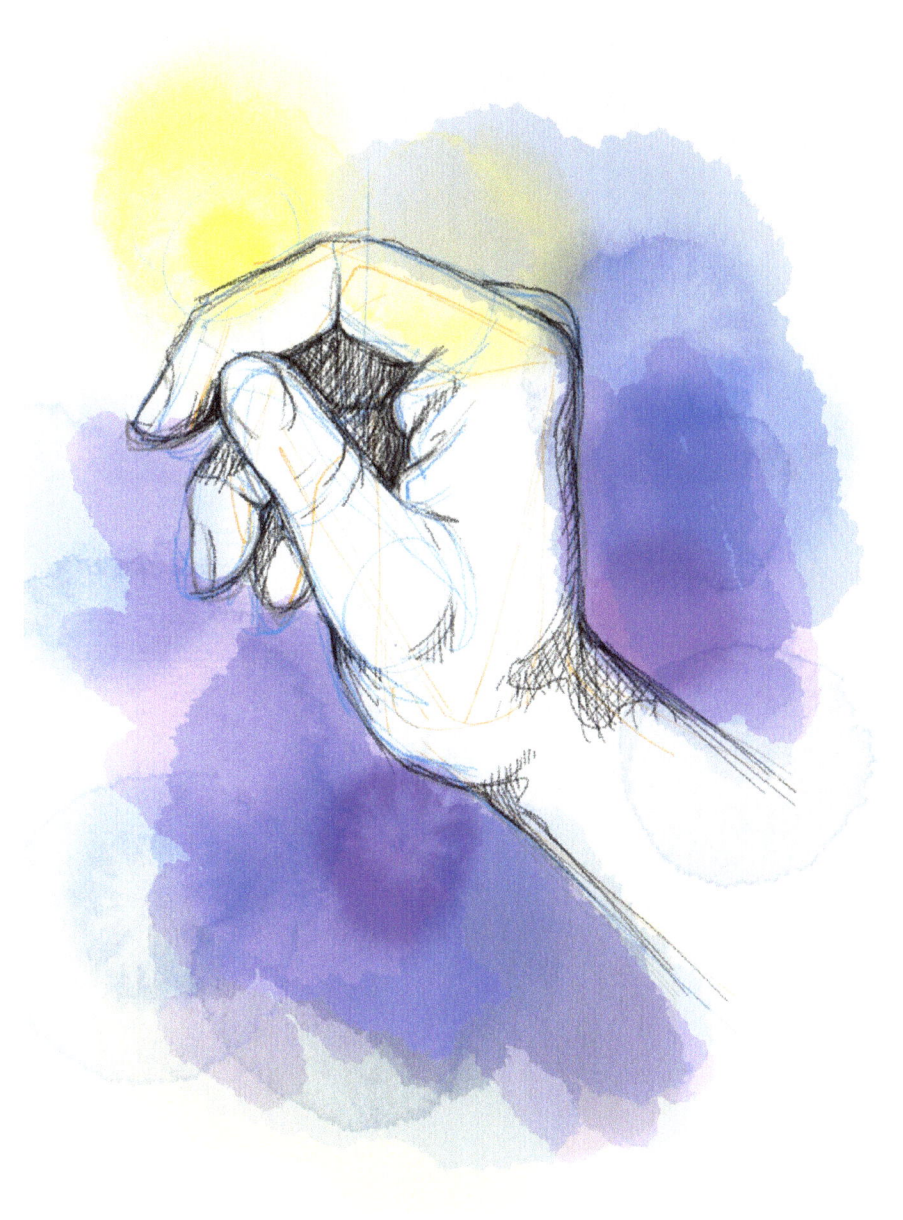

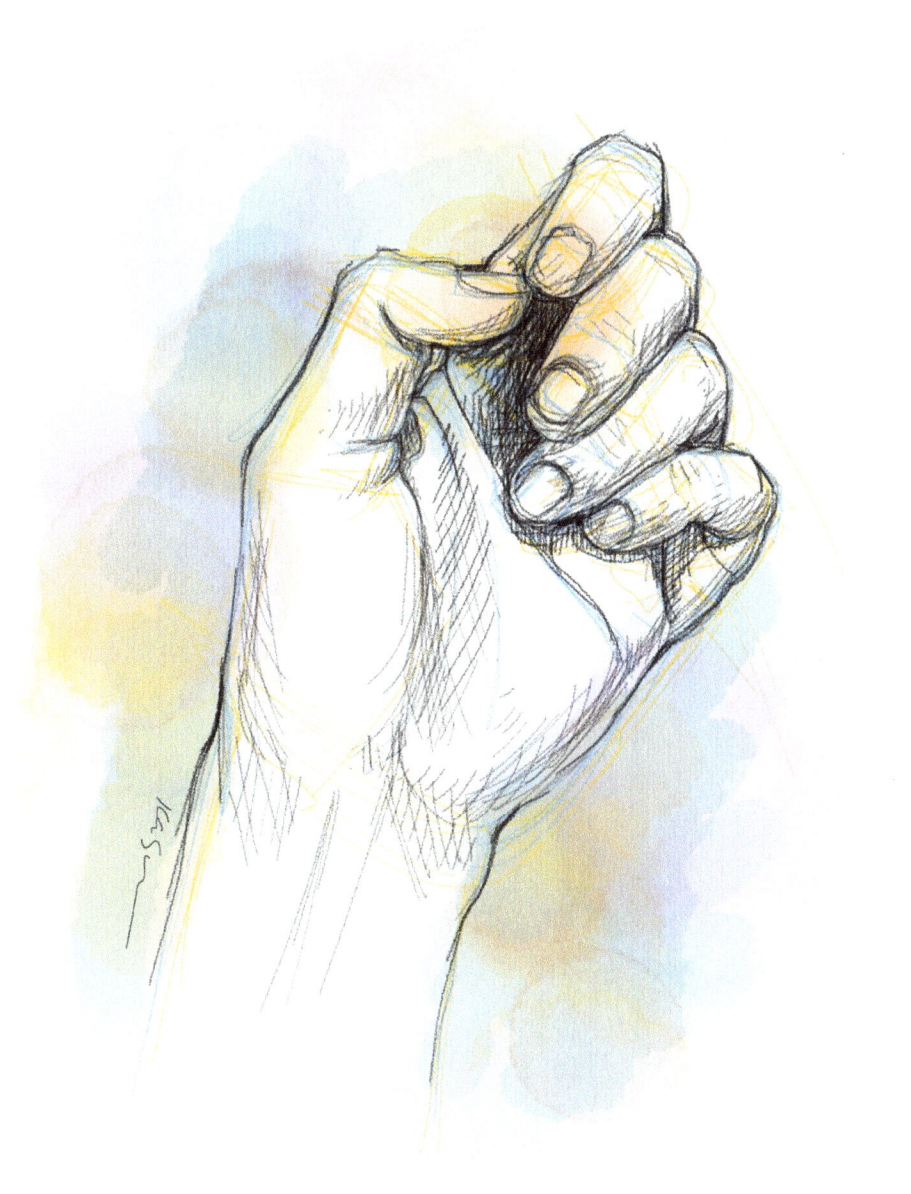

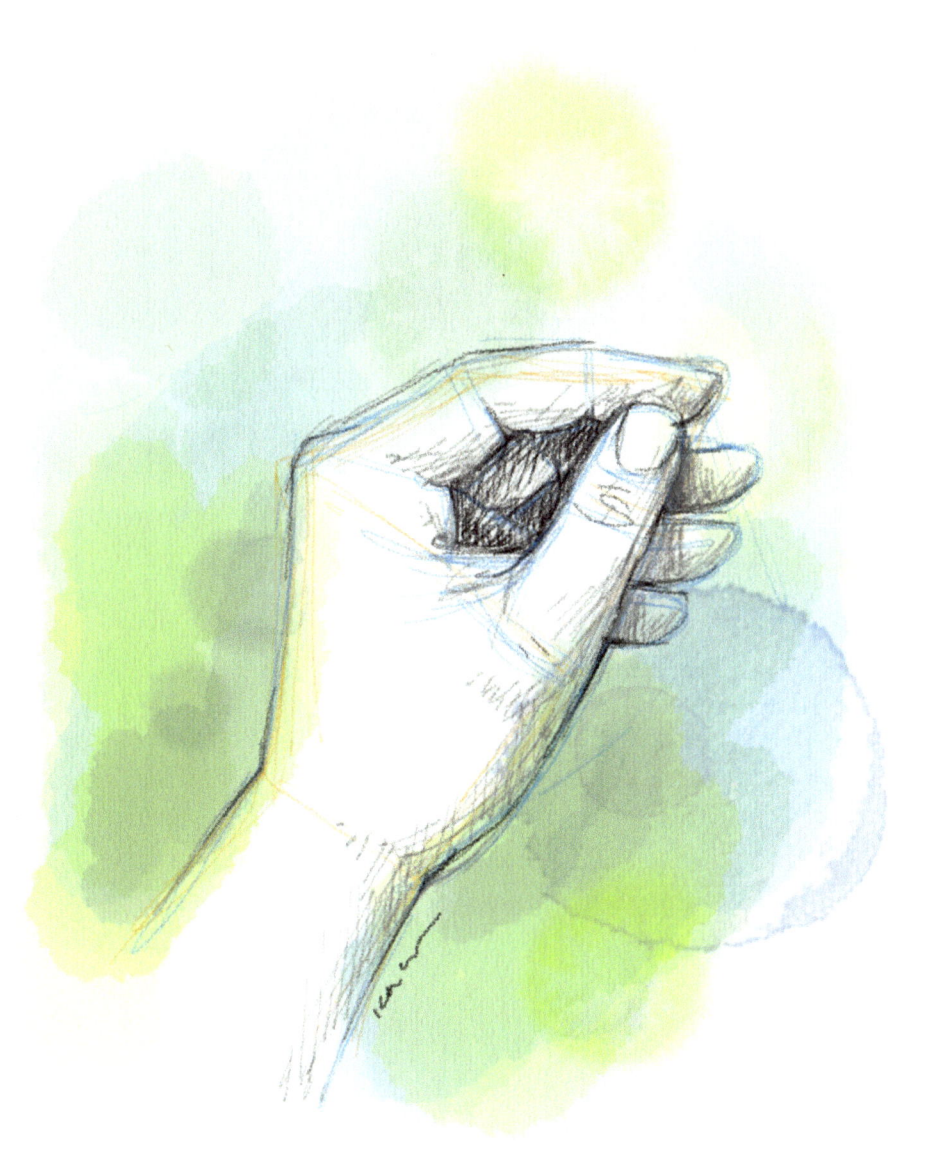

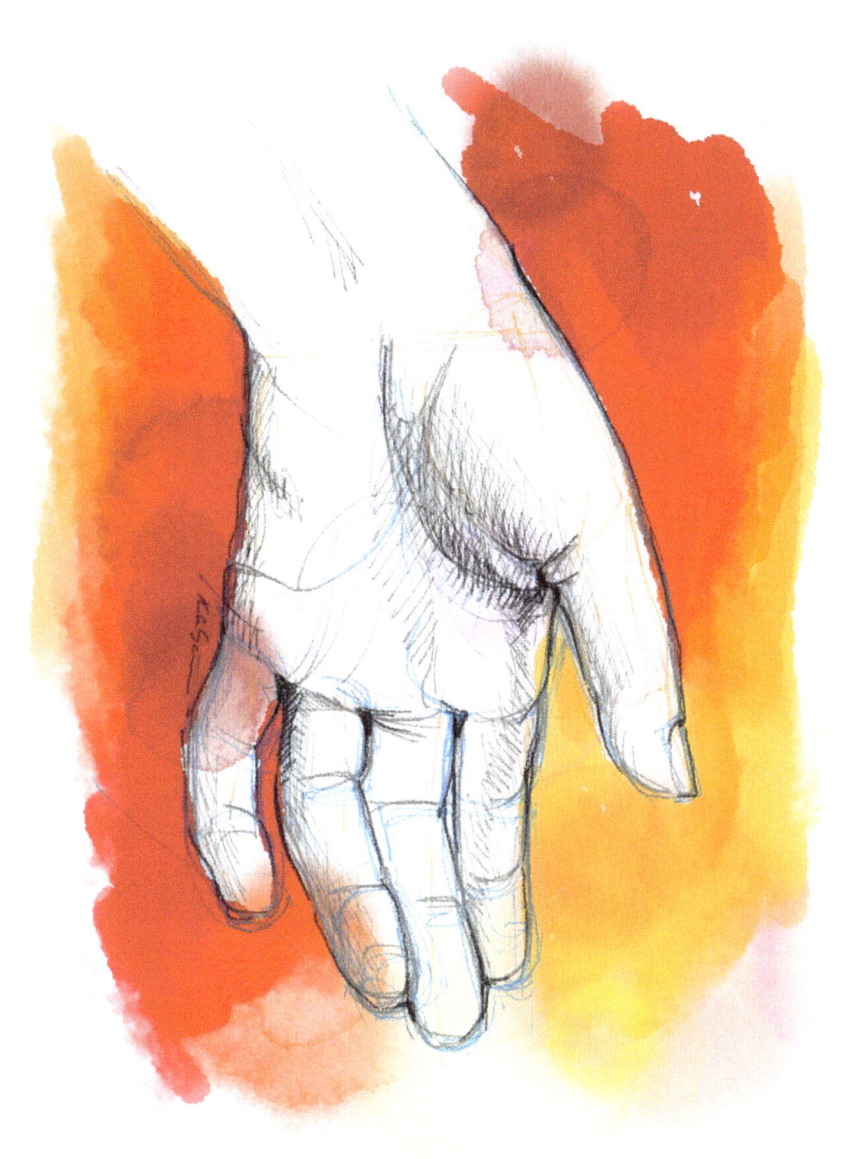

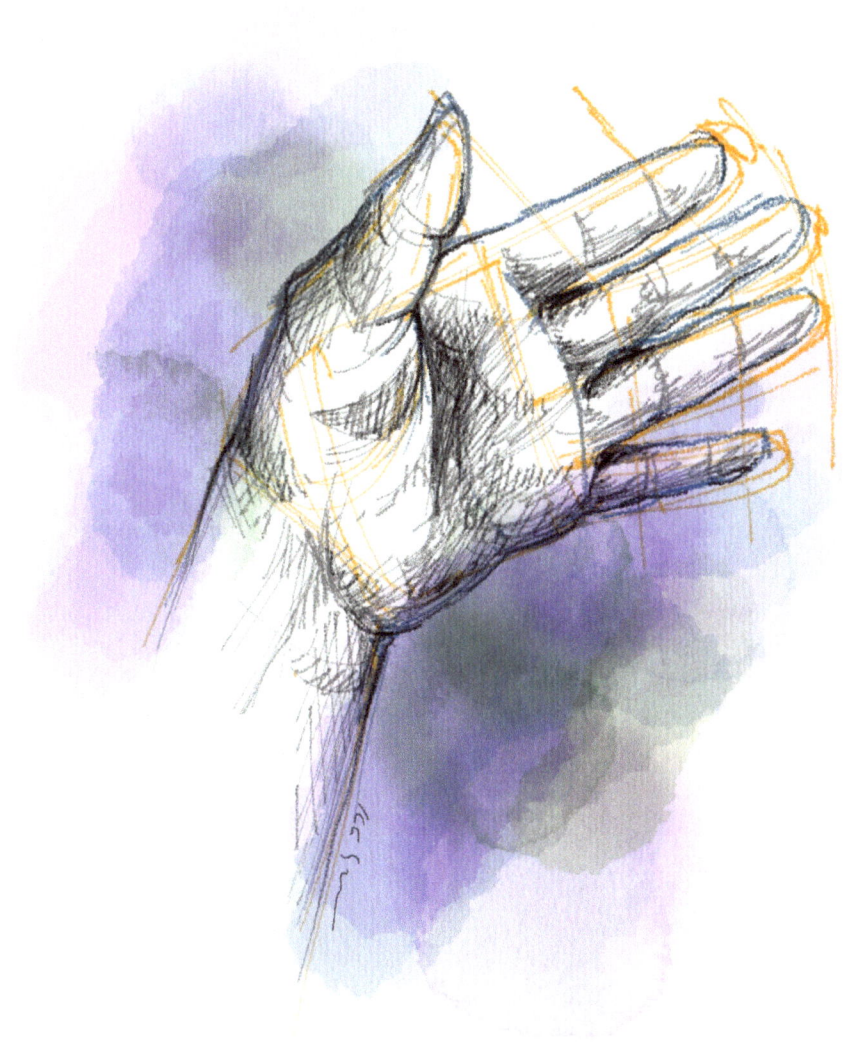

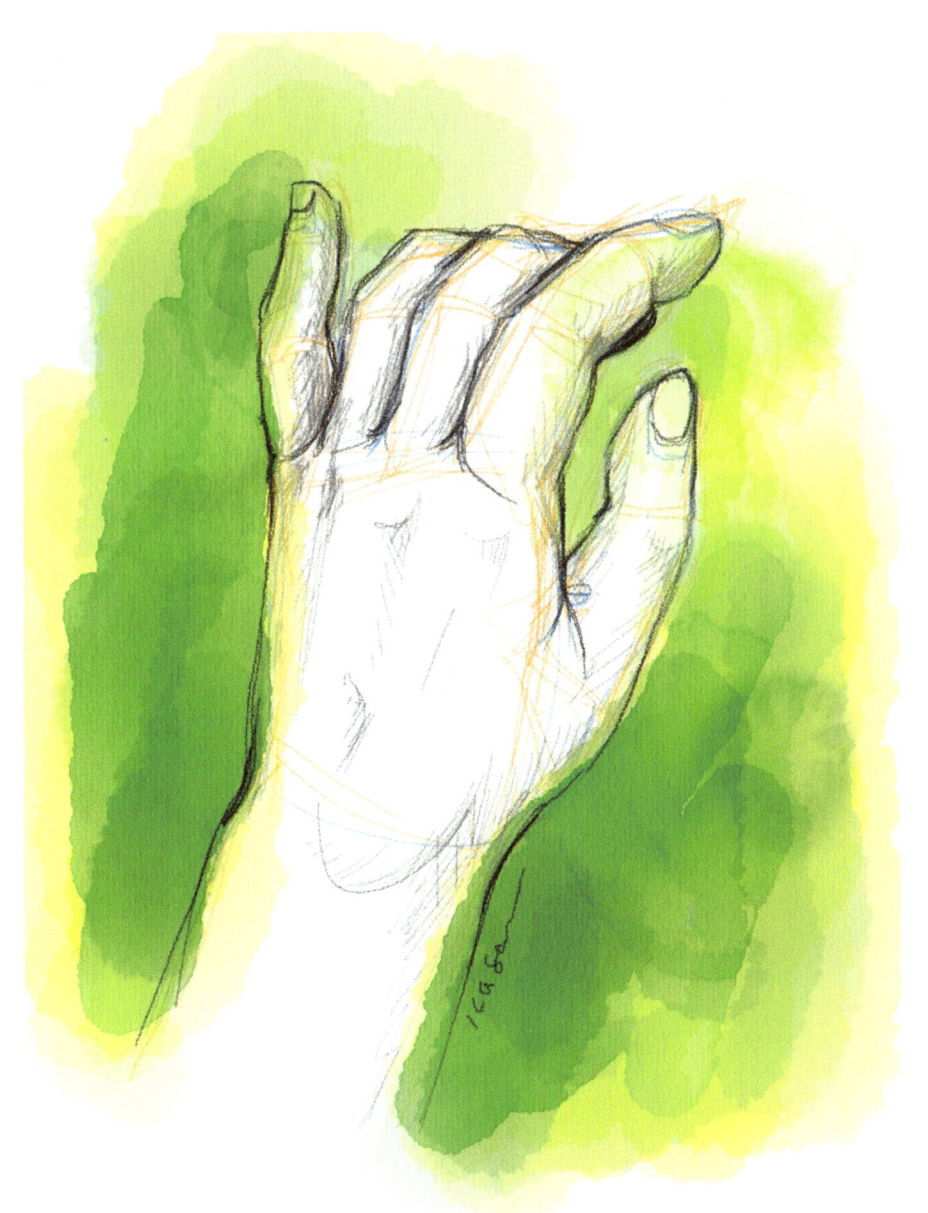

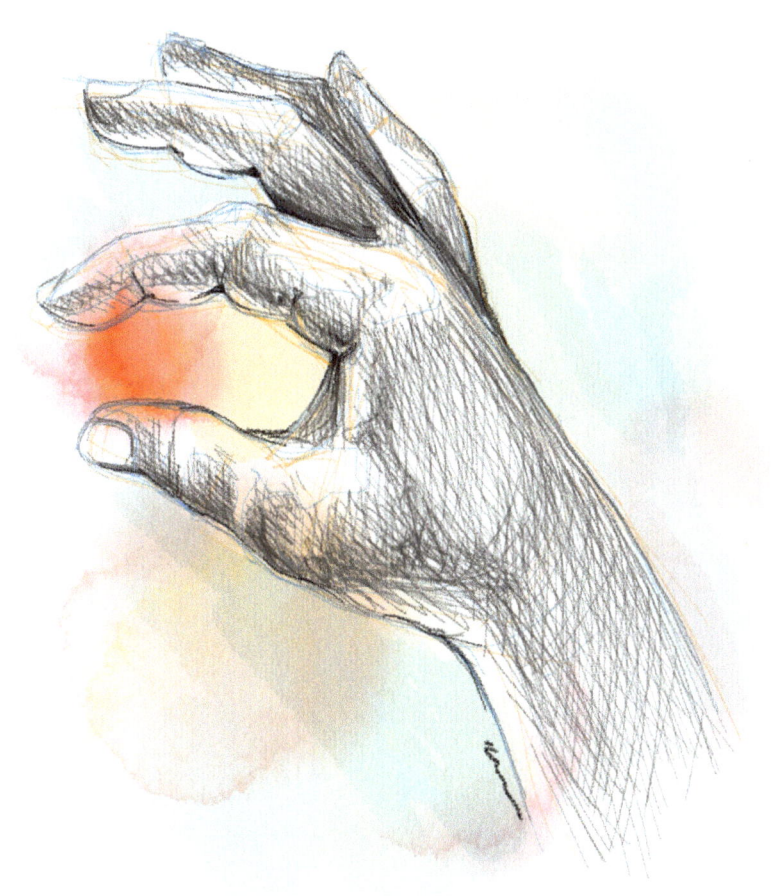

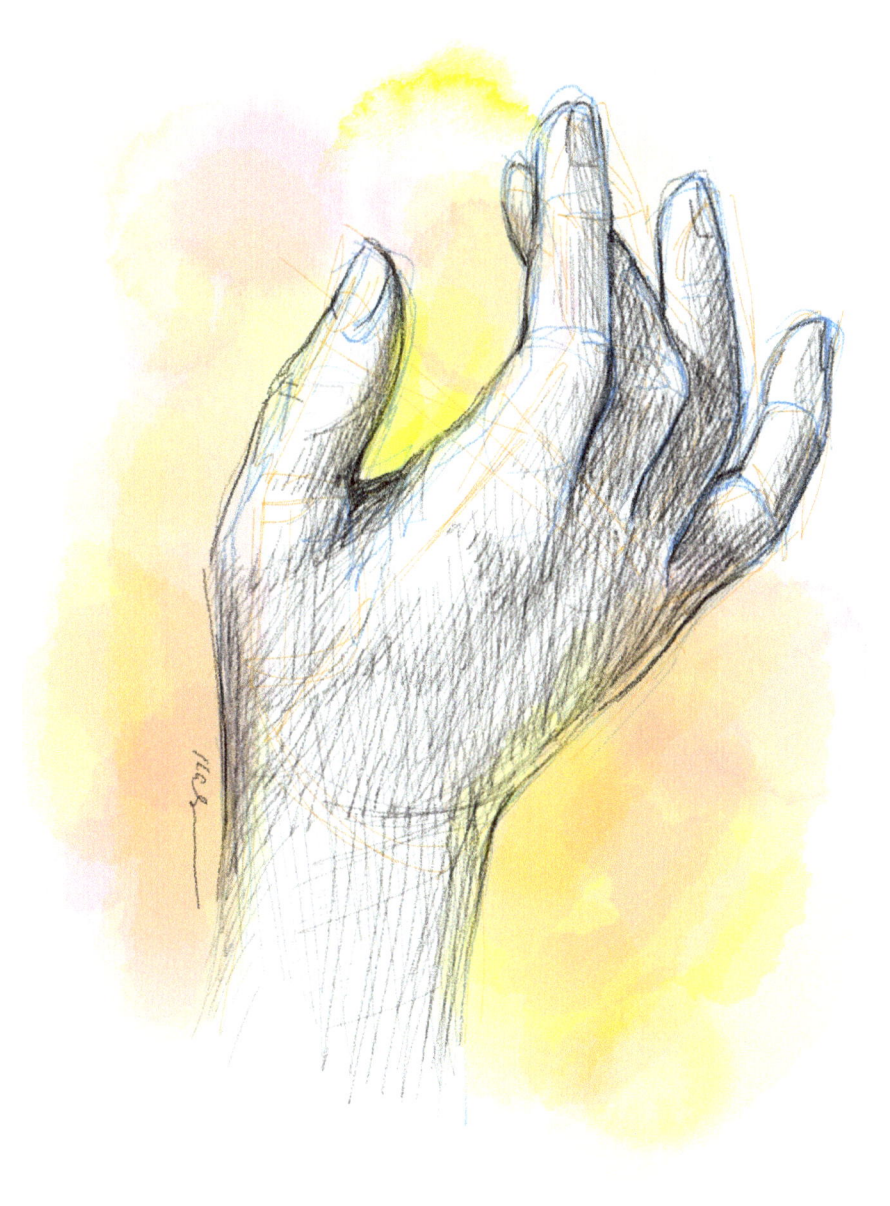

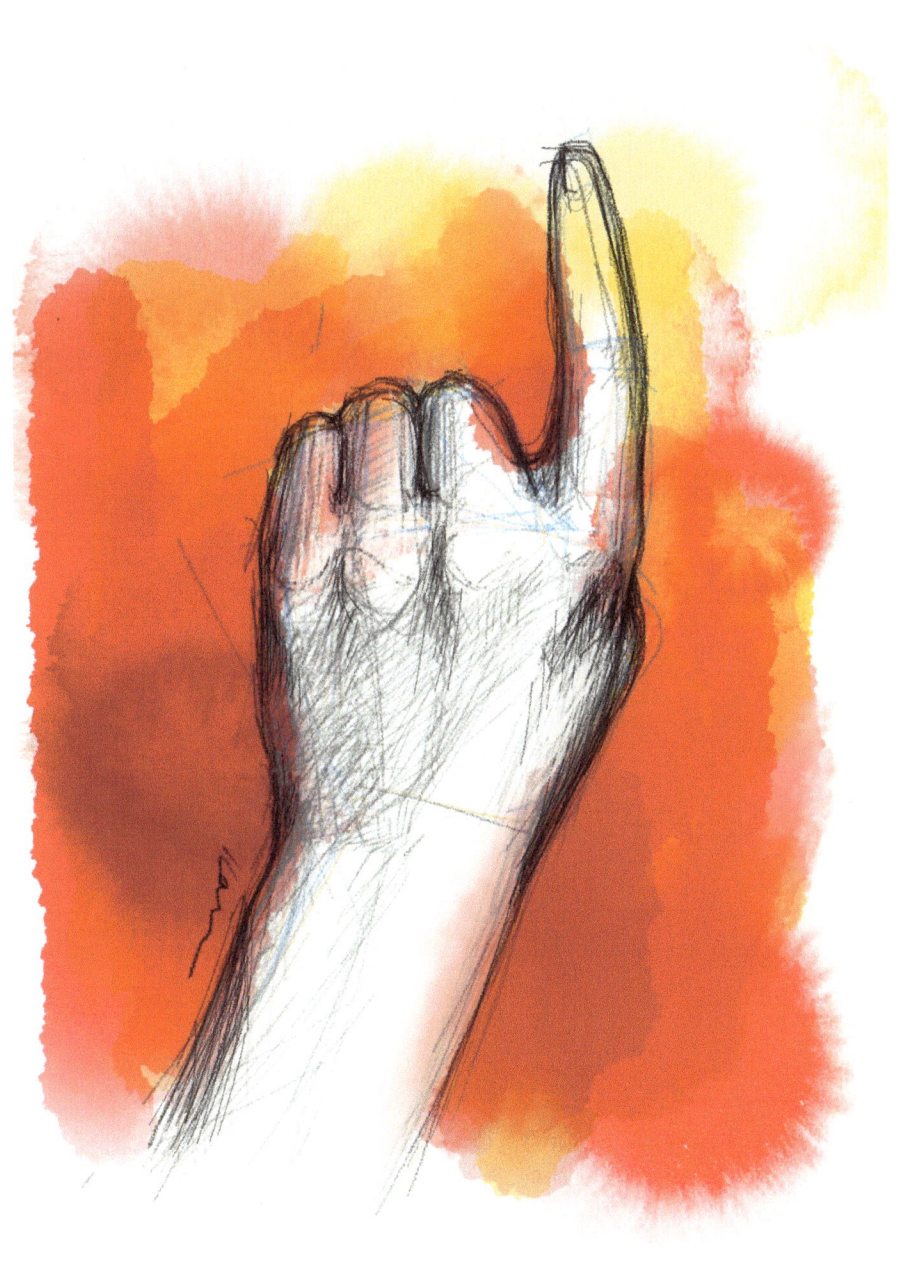

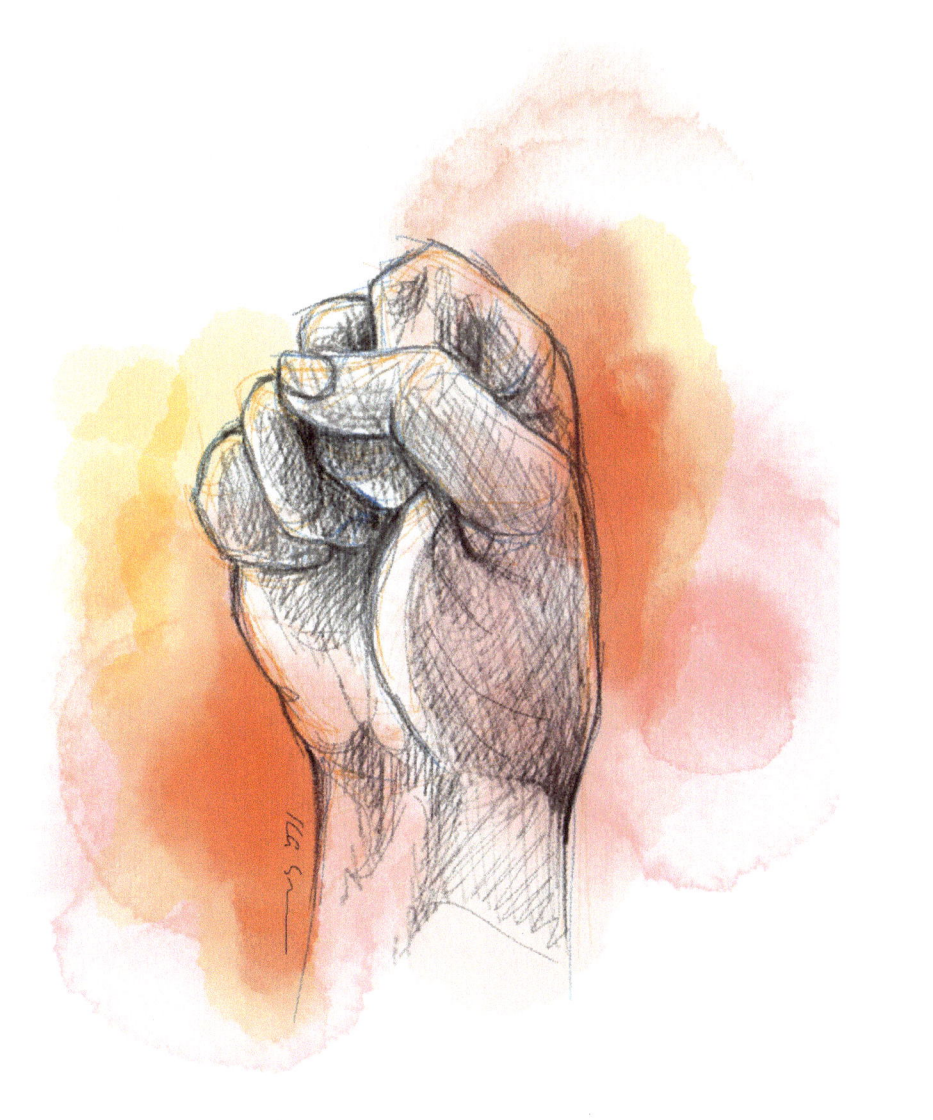

www.ingramcontent.com/pod-product-compliance
Lightning Source LLC
Chambersburg PA
CBHW040304220526
45473CB00002B/581